KS2 Success

Age 7-11

Times tables

Practice workbook

Angela Smith and Simon Greaves

About this book

Times tables

Times tables are an essential component of mathematics as they provide the building blocks for moving on to multiplication and division.

This book is designed to develop your child's times tables skills so that they can tackle them confidently and consistently at Key Stage 2. It will also aid preparation for the National Curriculum Test in mathematics (also known as SATs) at the end of Key Stage 2.

Work through the book with your child and encourage them to revisit their favourite activities or repeat the activities for a particular times table that may be posing problems. It is a good idea to reward your child with praise, encouragement and little treats for mastering all or part of a times table.

Features of the book

- *Learn your tables* – introduce the times tables and help understanding.

- *Parent's notes* – provide ideas for motivating your child and suggest extra activities to do in everyday life.

- *Tables practice and activities* – a variety of tasks and questions to engage your child.

- *Test your tables* – short tests to see how well your child knows the times table.

- *Speed tests and progress charts* – timed challenges to help your child master times tables. The progress charts enable both you and your child to monitor progress on a regular basis.

- *Answers* to all the questions are in a pull-out booklet at the centre of the book.

ACKNOWLEDGEMENTS

The author and publisher are grateful to the copyright holders for permission to use quoted materials and images.

P06 © Zubada; P08 © Tribalium; P12 © Tribalium; P16 © Tribalium; P18 © Matthew Cole; P20 © Tribalium; P24 © Tribalium; P26 © Paola Canzonetta; P28 © Tribalium; P47 © Matthew Cole, © Paola Canzonetta; P56 © elmm; P58 © elmm

The above images have been used under license from Shutterstock.com

All other images are ©Jupiterimages or © Letts Educational, an imprint of HarperCollinsPublishers Ltd

Every effort has been made to trace copyright holders and obtain their permission for the use of copyright material. The author and publisher will gladly receive information enabling them to rectify any error or omission in subsequent editions. All facts are correct at time of going to press.

Published by Letts Educational

An imprint of HarperCollinsPublishers Ltd
1 London Bridge Street
London SE1 9GF

ISBN 9781844198719

First published 2013

This edition published 2015

10 9 8 7 6 5 4 3 2 1

Text and Design ©Letts Educational, an imprint of HarperCollinsPublishers Ltd

British Library Cataloguing in Publication Data. A CIP record of this book is available from the British Library.

Commissioning Editor: Tammy Poggo

Authors: Angela Smith and Simon Greaves

Project Manager: Michelle I'Anson

Cover Design: Sarah Duxbury

Inside Concept Design: Ian Wrigley

Text, Design and Layout: Jouve India Private Limited

Printed and bound by RR Donnelley APS

Contents

2, 3, 4, 5 and 10 times tables

Learn your tables

By now you should be able to recall all of the multiplication facts in the two, three, four, five and ten times tables. You may notice that some multiplication facts are very alike.

For example: 3 × 5 = 15 and 5 × 3 = 15

You can also see that different multiplication facts give the same answer.

For example: 2 × 10 = 20 and 4 × 5 = 20

As well as knowing the answer to each multiplication it is also useful to know which number to multiply one by to get another.

For example, if you know 5 × 3 = 15 then you also know that the number to multiply 3 by to get 15 is 5.

The answers to the times tables are called multiples.

For example, the first twelve multiples of three are 3, 6, 9, 12, 15, 18, 21, 24, 27, 30, 33, 36.

Parent's note

Encourage your child to write out the times table or fill in a multiplication grid. Suggest your child race against a friend or do it alone racing against the clock – this can provide a real challenge that gets competitive-types going!

Don't forget to use correct times table vocabulary when you talk to your child (they will need to know the right language in the SATs). First of all, show them a multiplication fact, such as 6 × 4 = 24. Explain that 6 and 4 are factors of 24, and that 24 is a multiple of 6 and a multiple of 4.

Tables practice

1. Write in the missing number to complete each multiplication fact.

2 × 2 = ☐   ☐ × 10 = 90   12 × 5 = ☐

☐ × 3 = 12   9 × 2 = ☐   ☐ × 10 = 80

5 × 4 = ☐   ☐ × 3 = 21   7 × 2 = ☐

☐ × 5 = 35   6 × 4 = ☐   12 × 3 = ☐

2. Write in the missing number to complete each multiplication fact.

☐ × 4 = 48   3 × 3 = ☐   3 × 2 = ☐

☐ × 5 = 55   12 × 4 = ☐   ☐ × 3 = 15

7 × 10 = ☐   ☐ × 5 = 40   7 × 4 = ☐

☐ × 2 = 10   11 × 10 = ☐   ☐ × 5 = 45

Activities

1. Here is a machine that sorts numbers. Sort the numbers into multiples of three, four and five.

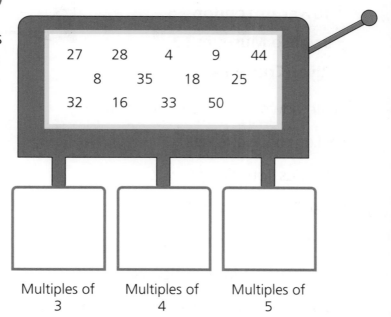

27   28   4   9   44
  8   35   18   25
32   16   33   50

Multiples of 3   Multiples of 4   Multiples of 5

2. Answer these questions.

What is 9 × 5? _____

What is the seventh multiple of 3? _____

What do you need to multiply 4 by to get 48? _____

What is the product of 6 and 10? _____

What is 8 × 2? _____

3. Shade a path through the number grid. Only shade multiples of five or ten.

13	27	54	90	70	15
62	76	41	5	17	68
33	19	72	45	11	88
3	20	55	80	7	19
81	50	21	57	78	99
25	40	53	71	44	9

→ Finish

Start →

4. Here are the ticket prices for places in London.

London Eye £10

Bus Tour £2

Tower of London £5

Science Museum £3

River Cruise £4

Write down how much it costs to buy:

Six London Eye tickets £ _____

Eight Bus Tour tickets £ _____

Seven River Cruise tickets £ _____

Five Tower of London tickets £ _____

Nine Science Museum tickets £ _____

How many River Cruise tickets could you buy for £48? _____

5. Count on or back to complete the number sequences.

48	44	☐	36	☐	☐	☐	20
3	☐	9	☐	☐	18	☐	☐
55	50	☐	☐	☐	☐	25	☐
120	110	☐	☐	☐	☐	☐	☐

6. Complete these multiplication facts.

4 × 3 = ☐   and   3 × 4 = ☐

2 × 10 = ☐   and   10 × 2 = ☐

5 × 3 = ☐   and   3 × 5 = ☐

☐ × 5 = 10   and   ☐ × 2 = 10

☐ × 2 = 8   and   ☐ × 4 = 8

☐ × 4 = 20   and   ☐ × 5 = 20

7. Complete the multiplication grid for the two, three, four, five and ten times tables.

×	2	3	4	5	10
1				5	
2	4				
3					30
4		12			
5	10				
6			24		
7					70
8	16				
9		27			
10				50	
11		33			
12			48		

Six times table

6

Learn your tables

You can use the three times table to help you with the six times table.

Just double all the answers.

You know that $7 \times 3 = 21$

Double it to get $7 \times 6 = 42$

All the answers in the six times table are even numbers.

1	×	6	=	6
2	×	6	=	12
3	×	6	=	18
4	×	6	=	24
5	×	6	=	30
6	×	6	=	36
7	×	6	=	42
8	×	6	=	48
9	×	6	=	54
10	×	6	=	60
11	×	6	=	66
12	×	6	=	72

Parent's note

Play 'guess my number' – someone thinks of a number and the others must guess the number by asking questions. For example, "Is it in the three times table?", "Is it odd?" Whoever guesses correctly thinks of the next number.

Tables practice

1. Write in the missing answer to complete each multiplication fact.

$7 \times 6 =$ ☐ $6 \times 6 =$ ☐ $9 \times 6 =$ ☐

$2 \times 6 =$ ☐ $10 \times 6 =$ ☐ $5 \times 6 =$ ☐

$12 \times 6 =$ ☐ $8 \times 6 =$ ☐ $11 \times 6 =$ ☐

$1 \times 6 =$ ☐ $3 \times 6 =$ ☐ $4 \times 6 =$ ☐

2. Write in the missing number to complete each multiplication fact.

☐ $\times 6 = 36$ ☐ $\times 6 = 30$ ☐ $\times 6 = 24$

☐ $\times 6 = 18$ ☐ $\times 6 = 54$ ☐ $\times 6 = 72$

☐ $\times 6 = 6$ ☐ $\times 6 = 12$ ☐ $\times 6 = 66$

☐ $\times 6 = 48$ ☐ $\times 6 = 42$ ☐ $\times 6 = 60$

Activities

1. A basket holds six kittens. Write a multiplication to show the number of kittens in the baskets.

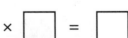

$5 \quad \times \quad 6 \quad = $ ☐

☐ $\times$ ☐ $=$ ☐

☐ $\times$ ☐ $=$ ☐

Six times table

2. Work out the answer to each times table fact to complete the grid.

5 × 6	
4 × 6	
8 × 6	
12 × 6	
7 × 6	
9 × 6	
3 × 6	

t
c
f
i
s
n
a

Using the code above, replace each of the numbers with the correct letters. What is the hidden word?

☐ ☐ ☐ ☐ ☐ ☐ ☐ ☐ ☐ !

48   18   54   30   18   42   30   72   24

3. Fill in the missing numbers by counting on or back in sixes.

12	☐	24	☐	36	☐	☐	☐
60	☐	48	☐	☐	30	☐	☐
18	☐	30	36	☐	☐	☐	☐
48	42	☐	☐	☐	☐	12	☐

4. Complete the multiplication facts for the scores on each target board.

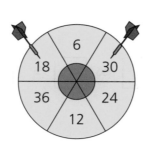

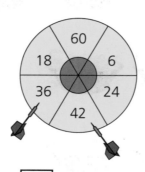

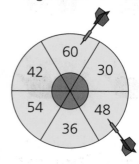

5 × 6 = 30

☐ × 6 = 18

☐ × 6 = 36

☐ × 6 = 42

☐ × 6 = 48

☐ × 6 = 60

Test your tables

1. Write out the six times table.

1 × 6 = ☐

2 × 6 = ☐

☐ × ☐ = ☐

☐ × ☐ = ☐

☐ × ☐ = ☐

☐ × ☐ = ☐

☐ × ☐ = ☐

☐ × ☐ = ☐

☐ × ☐ = ☐

☐ × ☐ = ☐

☐ × ☐ = ☐

☐ × ☐ = ☐

2. Complete these multiplication facts.

☐ × 6 = 18

12 × 6 = ☐

1 × 6 = ☐

☐ × 6 = 12

4 × 6 = ☐

☐ × 6 = 54

5 × 6 = ☐

7 × 6 = ☐

☐ × 6 = 36

☐ × 6 = 48

11 × 6 = ☐

☐ × 6 = 60

Score   /12

Score   /12

Seven times table

Learn your tables

The seven times table needs to be learned very carefully. It doesn't have any links with the other times tables.

1	×	7	=	7
2	×	7	=	14
3	×	7	=	21
4	×	7	=	28
5	×	7	=	35
6	×	7	=	42
7	×	7	=	49
8	×	7	=	56
9	×	7	=	63
10	×	7	=	70
11	×	7	=	77
12	×	7	=	84

Parent's note

Help your child to make a set of flash cards. Write a multiplication fact such as 4 × 7, on the front, and the answer, 28, on the back. The act of writing out each tables fact will provide another source of reinforcement. You can then use the cards to help your child learn the seven times table.

Tables practice

1. Write in the missing answer to complete each multiplication fact.

$9 \times 7 = \boxed{}$ $12 \times 7 = \boxed{}$ $5 \times 7 = \boxed{}$

$1 \times 7 = \boxed{}$ $2 \times 7 = \boxed{}$ $3 \times 7 = \boxed{}$

$10 \times 7 = \boxed{}$ $11 \times 7 = \boxed{}$ $7 \times 7 = \boxed{}$

$6 \times 7 = \boxed{}$ $4 \times 7 = \boxed{}$ $8 \times 7 = \boxed{}$

2. Write in the missing number to complete each multiplication fact.

$\boxed{} \times 7 = 77$ $\boxed{} \times 7 = 56$ $\boxed{} \times 7 = 70$

$\boxed{} \times 7 = 21$ $\boxed{} \times 7 = 28$ $\boxed{} \times 7 = 84$

$\boxed{} \times 7 = 42$ $\boxed{} \times 7 = 63$ $\boxed{} \times 7 = 49$

$\boxed{} \times 7 = 7$ $\boxed{} \times 7 = 14$ $\boxed{} \times 7 = 35$

Activities

1. Get the ball to the goal. You can only go through multiples of seven.
Shade the path you take.

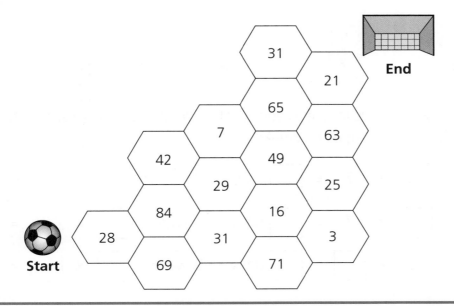

2. Complete the multiplication fact that describes each pattern.

$3 \times 7 = \boxed{}$

$\boxed{} \times 7 = \boxed{}$

$\boxed{} \times \boxed{} = \boxed{}$

$\boxed{} \times \boxed{} = \boxed{}$

3. Draw a line to match each multiplication to its answer.

(12 × 7)   (8 × 7)   (4 × 7)   (7 × 7)   (9 × 7)

| 28 | | 49 | | 84 | | 63 | | 56 |

4. There are seven days in one week. Write a multiplication to show the number of days for each number of weeks.

(5 weeks) $5 \times 7 = \boxed{}$ days   (8 weeks) $8 \times 7 = \boxed{}$ days

(3 weeks) $\boxed{} \times 7 = \boxed{}$ days   (4 weeks) $\boxed{} \times 7 = \boxed{}$ days

(7 weeks) $\boxed{} \times \boxed{} = \boxed{}$ days   (9 weeks) $\boxed{} \times \boxed{} = \boxed{}$ days

Test your tables

1. Write out the seven times table.

2. Complete these multiplication facts.

1 × 7 = ☐

12 × 7 = ☐

2 × 7 = ☐

☐ × 7 = 14

☐ × ☐ = ☐

☐ × 7 = 7

☐ × ☐ = ☐

8 × 7 = ☐

☐ × ☐ = ☐

☐ × 7 = 21

☐ × ☐ = ☐

4 × 7 = ☐

☐ × ☐ = ☐

7 × 7 = ☐

☐ × ☐ = ☐

6 × 7 = ☐

☐ × ☐ = ☐

☐ × 7 = 63

☐ × ☐ = ☐

☐ × 7 = 35

☐ × ☐ = ☐

☐ × 7 = 70

☐ × ☐ = ☐

11 × 7 = ☐

Score /12

Score /12

Eight times table

Learn your tables

By doubling all of the four times table facts you get the eight times table facts.

You know that $3 \times 4 = 12$

Double it to get $3 \times 8 = 24$

All the answers in the eight times table are even numbers.

$$1 \times 8 = 8$$
$$2 \times 8 = 16$$
$$3 \times 8 = 24$$
$$4 \times 8 = 32$$
$$5 \times 8 = 40$$
$$6 \times 8 = 48$$
$$7 \times 8 = 56$$
$$8 \times 8 = 64$$
$$9 \times 8 = 72$$
$$10 \times 8 = 80$$
$$11 \times 8 = 88$$
$$12 \times 8 = 96$$

Parent's note

Make up funny rhymes to help your child remember some of the more tricky tables. For example, for $8 \times 8 = 64$, "He ate and he ate so he stuck in the door, eight times eight is sixty-four".

Have a look at the 8 times table again. The unit digits have a regular pattern – they go down in twos: $1 \times 8 = 8$, $2 \times 8 = 16$, $3 \times 8 = 24$, $4 \times 8 = 32$.

Tables practice

1. Write in the missing answer to complete each multiplication fact.

$3 \times 8 = \boxed{}$ $1 \times 8 = \boxed{}$ $2 \times 8 = \boxed{}$

$5 \times 8 = \boxed{}$ $6 \times 8 = \boxed{}$ $8 \times 8 = \boxed{}$

$7 \times 8 = \boxed{}$ $10 \times 8 = \boxed{}$ $9 \times 8 = \boxed{}$

$11 \times 8 = \boxed{}$ $4 \times 8 = \boxed{}$ $12 \times 8 = \boxed{}$

2. Write in the missing number to complete each multiplication fact.

$\boxed{} \times 8 = 80$ $\boxed{} \times 8 = 24$ $\boxed{} \times 8 = 64$

$\boxed{} \times 8 = 32$ $\boxed{} \times 8 = 88$ $\boxed{} \times 8 = 56$

$\boxed{} \times 8 = 16$ $\boxed{} \times 8 = 40$ $\boxed{} \times 8 = 96$

$\boxed{} \times 8 = 72$ $\boxed{} \times 8 = 48$ $\boxed{} \times 8 = 8$

Activities

1. Shade a path through the number grid. Only shade answers that are in the eight times table.

12	15	66	24	80
30	76	28	16	63
47	4	54	56	36
18	22	88	64	75
26	49	40	17	9
48	72	96	59	37

Start →   ⟶ Finish

2. Some of these tables facts are correct and some are not. Tick those with correct answers. Put a cross next to those that are wrong.

7 × 8 = 66 ☐   9 × 8 = 72 ☐

5 × 8 = 40 ☐   10 × 8 = 70 ☐

8 × 8 = 64 ☐   6 × 8 = 48 ☐

3 × 8 = 26 ☐   2 × 8 = 16 ☐

3. An octopus has eight legs.

Write down how many legs there are on:

2 octopuses   2 × 8 = ☐

6 octopuses   ☐ × ☐ = ☐

8 octopuses   ☐ × ☐ = ☐

5 octopuses   ☐ × ☐ = ☐

There are 72 legs. How many octopuses are there? ☐

4. Which spider makes the number in the middle of the web when multiplied by eight? Colour the spider then complete the multiplication fact.

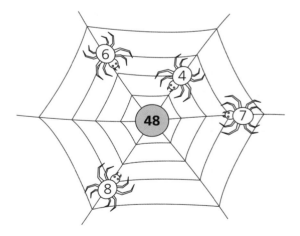

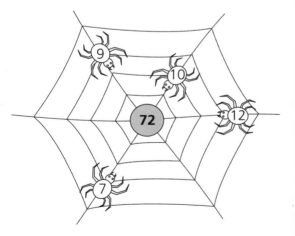

☐ × 8 = ☐   ☐ × 8 = ☐

Test your tables

1. Write out the eight times table.

1 × 8 = ☐

2 × 8 = ☐

☐ × ☐ = ☐

☐ × ☐ = ☐

☐ × ☐ = ☐

☐ × ☐ = ☐

☐ × ☐ = ☐

☐ × ☐ = ☐

☐ × ☐ = ☐

☐ × ☐ = ☐

☐ × ☐ = ☐

☐ × ☐ = ☐

2. Complete these multiplication facts.

☐ × 8 = 72

4 × 8 = ☐

7 × 8 = ☐

☐ × 8 = 16

12 × 8 = ☐

☐ × 8 = 88

3 × 8 = ☐

5 × 8 = ☐

☐ × 8 = 8

☐ × 8 = 48

8 × 8 = ☐

☐ × 8 = 80

Score /12

Score /12

Nine times table

Learn your tables

You can use your fingers to help learn the nine times table.

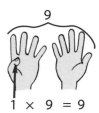
$1 \times 9 = 9$

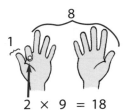
$2 \times 9 = 18$

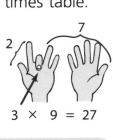
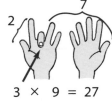
$3 \times 9 = 27$

1	×	9	=	9
2	×	9	=	18
3	×	9	=	27
4	×	9	=	36
5	×	9	=	45
6	×	9	=	54
7	×	9	=	63
8	×	9	=	72
9	×	9	=	81
10	×	9	=	90
11	×	9	=	99
12	×	9	=	108

Parent's note

With the exception of 11 × 9, all the answers in the nine times table have digits that add up to nine, for example, 9 × 9 = 81 and 8 + 1 = 9.

Buy some proper bingo dabbers and make simple bingo cards with multiples of nine on them. Call out a question, for example, "Nine nines?", and whoever has 81 dabs it. The person who gets a "full house" becomes the caller on the next round.

Tables practice

1. Write in the missing answer to complete each multiplication fact.

5 × 9 = ☐   7 × 9 = ☐   1 × 9 = ☐

8 × 9 = ☐   11 × 9 = ☐   6 × 9 = ☐

2 × 9 = ☐   4 × 9 = ☐   9 × 9 = ☐

3 × 9 = ☐   12 × 9 = ☐   10 × 9 = ☐

2. Write in the missing number to complete each multiplication fact.

☐ × 9 = 45   ☐ × 9 = 63   ☐ × 9 = 36

☐ × 9 = 18   ☐ × 9 = 27   ☐ × 9 = 81

☐ × 9 = 9   ☐ × 9 = 54   ☐ × 9 = 90

☐ × 9 = 99   ☐ × 9 = 108   ☐ × 9 = 72

Activities

1. Each tree has nine apples. Write a multiplication to show the number of apples on the trees.

7 × 9 = ☐

☐ × ☐ = ☐

☐ × ☐ = ☐

☐ × ☐ = ☐

Nine times table

2. Every number put into the machine is multiplied by 9.

Write in the missing numbers.

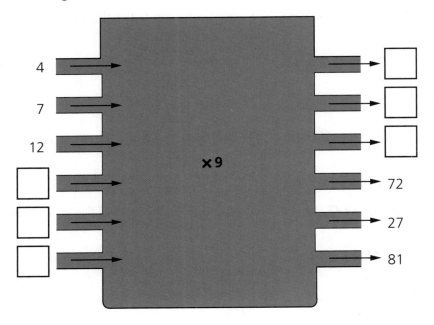

3. Fill in the missing numbers by counting on or back in nines.

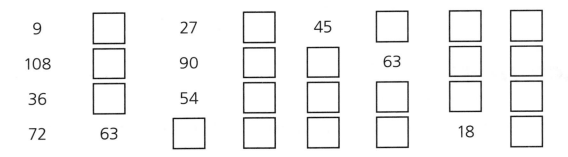

4. Work out the answer to the multiplication in each circle. Use your answers to fill in the missing letters in the spaces below. What is the hidden message?

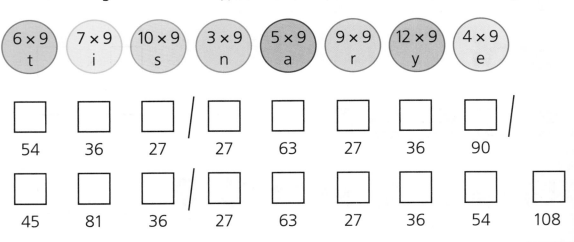

Test your tables

1. Write out the nine times table.

1 × 9 = ☐

2 × 9 = ☐

☐ × ☐ = ☐

☐ × ☐ = ☐

☐ × ☐ = ☐

☐ × ☐ = ☐

☐ × ☐ = ☐

☐ × ☐ = ☐

☐ × ☐ = ☐

☐ × ☐ = ☐

☐ × ☐ = ☐

☐ × ☐ = ☐

2. Complete these multiplication facts.

☐ × 9 = 27

6 × 9 = ☐

☐ × 9 = 81

1 × 9 = ☐

☐ × 9 = 36

☐ × 9 = 90

12 × 9 = ☐

7 × 9 = ☐

2 × 9 = ☐

☐ × 9 = 72

5 × 9 = ☐

☐ × 9 = 99

Score   /12

Score   /12

Eleven times table

Learn your tables

Notice that to find the first nine answers in the eleven times table, you simply write the digit you are multiplying by twice. After this it gets a bit trickier! You'll need to learn the last three off by heart.

1	×	11	=	11
2	×	11	=	22
3	×	11	=	33
4	×	11	=	44
5	×	11	=	55
6	×	11	=	66
7	×	11	=	77
8	×	11	=	88
9	×	11	=	99
10	×	11	=	110
11	×	11	=	121
12	×	11	=	132

Parent's note

Try saying the eleven times table aloud in a rhythm as you walk or drive to school. Perhaps begin by taking it in turns to work through the table, for example, you say, "Two times eleven is twenty-two," your child says, "Three times eleven is thirty-three"...

Tables practice

1. Write in the missing answer to complete each multiplication fact.

5 × 11 = ☐   9 × 11 = ☐   6 × 11 = ☐

7 × 11 = ☐   11 × 11 = ☐   2 × 11 = ☐

4 × 11 = ☐   8 × 11 = ☐   12 × 11 = ☐

1 × 11 = ☐   10 × 11 = ☐   3 × 11 = ☐

2. Write in the missing number to complete each multiplication fact.

☐ × 11 = 66   ☐ × 11 = 33   ☐ × 11 = 77

☐ × 11 = 22   ☐ × 11 = 88   ☐ × 11 = 132

☐ × 11 = 44   ☐ × 11 = 121   ☐ × 11 = 110

☐ × 11 = 55   ☐ × 11 = 99   ☐ × 11 = 11

Activities

1. A packet of crisps costs 11p. Write down how much it costs for each number of packets.

   7   ×   11   =   ☐ p

   4   ×   ☐   =   ☐ p

   ☐   ×   ☐   =   ☐ p

Eleven times table

2. There are 11 footballers in a team. Write multiplications to show the number of footballers for each number of teams.

4 teams	4	×	11	= ☐
9 teams	9	×	☐	= ☐
5 teams	☐	×	☐	= ☐
8 teams	☐	×	☐	= ☐

3. Answer these questions.

What is 6 multiplied by 11? _____

What is the product of 9 and 11? _____

How many elevens are in 44? _____

What do you need to multiply 11 by to get 110? _____

What is the fifth multiple of 11? _____

What is 11 multiplied by itself? _____

4. In the box at the bottom of each mountain, write down the number that multiplies by eleven to give the number at the top of the mountain.

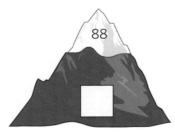

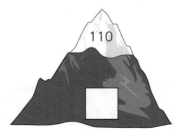

Test your tables

1. Write out the eleven times table.

2. Complete these multiplication facts.

1 × 11 = ☐

☐ × 11 = 55

2 × 11 = ☐

8 × 11 = ☐

☐ × ☐ = ☐

☐ × 11 = 66

☐ × ☐ = ☐

10 × 11 = ☐

☐ × ☐ = ☐

7 × 11 = ☐

☐ × ☐ = ☐

☐ × 11 = 11

☐ × ☐ = ☐

☐ × 11 = 121

☐ × ☐ = ☐

4 × 11 = ☐

☐ × ☐ = ☐

☐ × 11 = 132

☐ × ☐ = ☐

9 × 11 = ☐

☐ × ☐ = ☐

3 × 11 = ☐

☐ × ☐ = ☐

☐ × 11 = 22

Score   /12

Score   /12

Twelve times table

Learn your tables

You can work out the twelve times table by doubling the six times table.

You know that 4 × **6** = **24**

Double it to get 4 × **12** = **48**

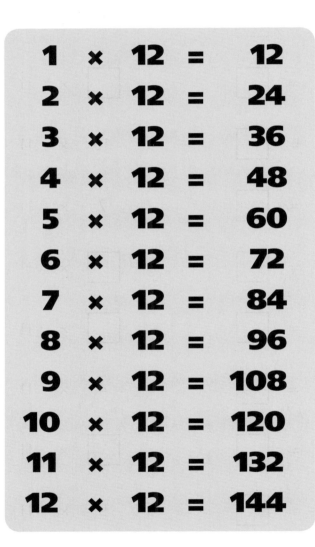

$$1 \times 12 = 12$$
$$2 \times 12 = 24$$
$$3 \times 12 = 36$$
$$4 \times 12 = 48$$
$$5 \times 12 = 60$$
$$6 \times 12 = 72$$
$$7 \times 12 = 84$$
$$8 \times 12 = 96$$
$$9 \times 12 = 108$$
$$10 \times 12 = 120$$
$$11 \times 12 = 132$$
$$12 \times 12 = 144$$

Parent's note

If your child is struggling with the twelve times table, suggest that they try finding the answers by adding together multiples of 10 and multiples of 2.

For example, to work out 4 × 12, work out 4 × 10 and add to 4 × 2.

Tables practice

1. Write in the missing answer to complete each multiplication fact.

$3 \times 12 = \boxed{}$

$6 \times 12 = \boxed{}$

$9 \times 12 = \boxed{}$

$8 \times 12 = \boxed{}$

$10 \times 12 = \boxed{}$

$12 \times 12 = \boxed{}$

$11 \times 12 = \boxed{}$

$4 \times 12 = \boxed{}$

$2 \times 12 = \boxed{}$

$1 \times 12 = \boxed{}$

$7 \times 12 = \boxed{}$

$5 \times 12 = \boxed{}$

2. Write in the missing number to complete each multiplication fact.

$\boxed{} \times 12 = 108$

$\boxed{} \times 12 = 24$

$\boxed{} \times 12 = 132$

$\boxed{} \times 12 = 48$

$\boxed{} \times 12 = 60$

$\boxed{} \times 12 = 36$

$\boxed{} \times 12 = 72$

$\boxed{} \times 12 = 12$

$\boxed{} \times 12 = 84$

$\boxed{} \times 12 = 144$

$\boxed{} \times 12 = 120$

$\boxed{} \times 12 = 96$

Activities

1. Sanjay wants to cross the playground from his school to the gate. He can only walk on the paving stones that are multiples of 12. Shade the path he needs to take.

End

27	58	73	31	72	144	84
37	64	105	96	60	59	127
42	122	86	31	120	26	121
58	48	108	132	24	106	134
16	60	92	117	125	93	126
12	36	49	111	14	20	76

Start

Twelve times table

2. Every number put into the machine is multiplied by 12.
Fill in the missing numbers.

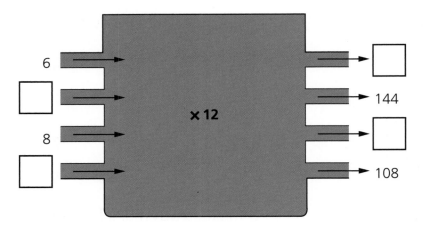

3. Answer these questions.

What is 12 multiplied by 6?   _____

Which number multiplied by 12 gives 84?   _____

What is 12 multiplied by itself?   _____

What is the product of 12 and 5?   _____

4. Here is Jack's homework. Mark his homework by putting a tick next to those with the correct answer and a cross next to those with the wrong answer.

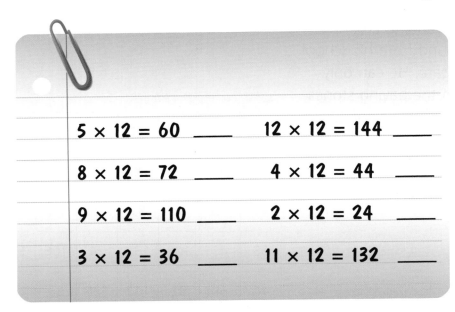

$5 \times 12 = 60$ ____ $12 \times 12 = 144$ ____

$8 \times 12 = 72$ ____ $4 \times 12 = 44$ ____

$9 \times 12 = 110$ ____ $2 \times 12 = 24$ ____

$3 \times 12 = 36$ ____ $11 \times 12 = 132$ ____

Answers

2, 3, 4, 5 and 10 times tables

Tables practice
1. 4, 9, 60, 4, 18, 8, 20, 7, 14, 7, 24, 36
2. 12, 9, 6, 11, 48, 5, 70, 8, 28, 5, 110, 9

Activities
1. Multiples of 3 – 9, 18, 27, 33;
    Multiples of 4 – 4, 8, 16, 28, 32, 44;
    Multiples of 5 – 25, 35, 50
2. 45, 21, 12, 60, 16
3. Shade 25, 40, 50, 20, 55, 80, 45, 5, 90,
    70, 15
4. £60, £16, £28, £25, £27, 12
5. 40, 32, 28, 24;
    6, 12, 15, 21, 24;
    45, 40, 35, 30, 20;
    100, 90, 80, 70, 60, 50
6. 12, 12, 20, 20, 15, 15, 2, 5, 4, 2, 5, 4
7. (×1) 2, 3, 4, 10; (×2) 6, 8, 10, 20;
    (×3) 6, 9, 12, 15; (×4) 8, 16, 20, 40;
    (×5) 15, 20, 25, 50; (×6) 12, 18, 30, 60;
    (×7) 14, 21, 28, 35; (×8) 24, 32, 40, 80;
    (×9) 18, 36, 45, 90; (×10) 20, 30, 40, 100;
    (×11) 22, 44, 55, 110; (×12) 24, 36, 60, 120

Six times table

Tables practice
1. 42, 36, 54, 12, 60, 30, 72, 48, 66, 6, 18, 24
2. 6, 5, 4, 3, 9, 12, 1, 2, 11, 8, 7, 10

Activities
1. 30, 4 × 6 = 24, 7 × 6 = 42
2. fantastic!
3. 18, 30, 42, 48, 54;
    54, 42, 36, 24, 18;
    24, 42, 48, 54, 60;
    36, 30, 24, 18, 6
4. First board: 3; Second board: 6, 7;
    Third board: 8, 10

Test your tables
1. 1 × 6 = 6, 2 × 6 = 12, 3 × 6 = 18,
    4 × 6 = 24, 5 × 6 = 30, 6 × 6 = 36,
    7 × 6 = 42, 8 × 6 = 48, 9 × 6 = 54,
    10 × 6 = 60, 11 × 6 = 66, 12 × 6 = 72
2. 3, 72, 6, 2, 24, 9, 30, 42, 6, 8, 66, 10

Seven times table

Tables practice
1. 63, 84, 35, 7, 14, 21, 70, 77, 49, 42, 28, 56
2. 11, 8, 10, 3, 4, 12, 6, 9, 7, 1, 2, 5

Activities
1. Shade 28, 84, 42, 7, 49, 63, 21
2. 21, 4 × 7 = 28, 5 × 7 = 35, 6 × 7 = 42
3. 12 × 7 and 84, 8 × 7 and 56, 4 × 7 and
    28, 7 × 7 and 49, 9 × 7 and 63
4. 35, 56, 3 × 7 = 21, 4 × 7 = 28,
    7 × 7 = 49, 9 × 7 = 63

Test your tables
1. 1 × 7 = 7, 2 × 7 = 14, 3 × 7 = 21,
    4 × 7 = 28, 5 × 7 = 35, 6 × 7 = 42,
    7 × 7 = 49, 8 × 7 = 56, 9 × 7 = 63,
    10 × 7 = 70, 11 × 7 = 77, 12 × 7 = 84
2. 84, 2, 1, 56, 3, 28, 49, 42, 9, 5, 10, 77

Eight times table

Tables practice
1. 24, 8, 16, 40, 48, 64, 56, 80, 72, 88,
    32, 96
2. 10, 3, 8, 4, 11, 7, 2, 5, 12, 9, 6, 1

Activities
1. Shade 48, 72, 96, 40, 88, 64, 56, 16,
    24, 80
2. ✗, ✔, ✔, ✗, ✔, ✔, ✗, ✔
3. 16, 6 × 8 = 48, 8 × 8 = 64, 5 × 8 = 40,
    9 octopuses
4. Colour spider 6, 6 × 8 = 48;
    Colour spider 9, 9 × 8 = 72

Test your tables
1. 1 × 8 = 8, 2 × 8 = 16, 3 × 8 = 24,
    4 × 8 = 32, 5 × 8 = 40, 6 × 8 = 48,
    7 × 8 = 56, 8 × 8 = 64, 9 × 8 = 72,
    10 × 8 = 80, 11 × 8 = 88, 12 × 8 = 96
2. 9, 32, 56, 2, 96, 11, 24, 40, 1, 6,
    64, 10

Nine times table

Tables practice
1. 45, 63, 9, 72, 99, 54, 18, 36, 81, 27,
    108, 90
2. 5, 7, 4, 2, 3, 9, 1, 6, 10, 11, 12, 8

Answers

Activities
1. 63, 2 × 9 = 18, 5 × 9 = 45, 8 × 9 = 72
2. Numbers down left: 8, 3, 9
   Numbers down right: 36, 63, 108
3. 18, 36, 54, 63, 72;
   99, 81, 72, 54, 45;
   45, 63, 72, 81, 90, 99;
   54, 45, 36, 27, 9
4. ten nines are ninety

Test your tables
1. 1 × 9 = 9, 2 × 9 = 18, 3 × 9 = 27,
   4 × 9 = 36, 5 × 9 = 45, 6 × 9 = 54,
   7 × 9 = 63, 8 × 9 = 72, 9 × 9 = 81,
   10 × 9 = 90, 11 × 9 = 99, 12 × 9 = 108
2. 3, 54, 9, 9, 4, 10, 108, 63, 18, 8, 45, 11

Eleven times table

Tables practice
1. 55, 99, 66, 77, 121, 22, 44, 88, 132, 11,
   110, 33
2. 6, 3, 7, 2, 8, 12, 4, 11, 10, 5, 9, 1

Activities
1. 77p, 4 × 11 = 44p, 6 × 11 = 66p
2. 44, 9 × 11 = 99, 5 × 11 = 55, 8 × 11 = 88
3. 66, 99, 4, 10, 55, 121
4. 8, 12, 3, 10

Test your tables
1. 1 × 11 = 11, 2 × 11 = 22, 3 × 11 = 33,
   4 × 11 = 44, 5 × 11 = 55, 6 × 11 = 66,
   7 × 11 = 77, 8 × 11 = 88, 9 × 11 = 99,
   10 × 11 = 110, 11 × 11 = 121, 12 × 11 = 132
2. 5, 88, 6, 110, 77, 1, 11, 44, 12, 99,
   33, 2

Twelve times table

Tables practice
1. 36, 120, 24, 72, 144, 12, 108, 132, 84,
   96, 48, 60
2. 9, 5, 7, 2, 3, 12, 11, 6, 10, 4, 1, 8

Activities
1. Shade 12, 36, 60, 48, 108, 132, 24, 120,
   60, 72, 144, 84
2. Numbers down left: 12, 9
   Numbers down right: 72, 96
3. 72, 7, 144, 60
4. ✔, ✔, ✗, ✗, ✗, ✔, ✔, ✔

Test your tables
1. 1 × 12 = 12, 2 × 12 = 24, 3 × 12 = 36,
   4 × 12 = 48, 5 × 12 = 60, 6 × 12 = 72,
   7 × 12 = 84, 8 × 12 = 96, 9 × 12 = 108,
   10 × 12 = 120, 11 × 12 = 132,
   12 × 12 = 144
2. 5, 48, 24, 120, 144, 9, 6, 96, 7, 1, 36, 11

Three, six and nine times tables

Tables practice
1. 1 × 3 = 3, 2 × 3 = 6, 3 × 3 = 9,
   4 × 3 = 12, 5 × 3 = 15, 6 × 3 = 18,
   7 × 3 = 21, 8 × 3 = 24, 9 × 3 = 27,
   10 × 3 = 30, 11 × 3 = 33,
   12 × 3 = 36
2. 1 × 6 = 6, 2 × 6 = 12, 3 × 6 = 18,
   4 × 6 = 24, 5 × 6 = 30, 6 × 6 = 36,
   7 × 6 = 42, 8 × 6 = 48, 9 × 6 = 54,
   10 × 6 = 60, 11 × 6 = 66, 12 × 6 = 72
3. 1 × 9 = 9, 2 × 9 = 18, 3 × 9 = 27,
   4 × 9 = 36, 5 × 9 = 45, 6 × 9 = 54,
   7 × 9 = 63, 8 × 9 = 72, 9 × 9 = 81,
   10 × 9 = 90, 11 × 9 = 99, 12 × 9 = 108
4. 18, 4, 90, 12, 30, 12, 45, 6, 11, 5, 81, 24,
   2, 42, 2

Activities
1. First pyramid: 7 × 9, 7 × 3, 9 × 9,
   5 × 3, 12 × 9; Second pyramid: 54, 42,
   36, 60
2. Colour 24, 45, 63, 72, 30, 54, 108, 27
3. 18, 63, 9, 81, 12, 36
4. £24, £42, £36, £15, £72, £99, 12, 9, 12
5. First board: 7; Second board: 10, 8;
   Third board: 9, 12
6. 15, 18, 24, 30;
   36, 54, 63, 81;
   36, 30, 27, 24, 18;
   72, 63, 45, 27;
   24, 36, 42, 54;
   72, 60, 54, 48, 36
7. 24, 36, 81, 18, 18, 108, 42, 18,
   letters spell out EIGHTEEN
8. 7 × 3 and 21, 8 × 6 and 48, 7 × 9 and
   63, 12 × 3 and 36, 4 × 6 and 24, 12 × 9
   and 108, 12 × 6 and 72

9. (1) 48, (2) 81, (3) 12, (4) 24, (5) 45, (6) 54, (7) 42, (8) 27, (9) 72, (10) 21

Four, eight and twelve times tables

Tables practice

1. $1 \times 4 = 4$, $2 \times 4 = 8$, $3 \times 4 = 12$, $4 \times 4 = 16$, $5 \times 4 = 20$, $6 \times 4 = 24$, $7 \times 4 = 28$, $8 \times 4 = 32$, $9 \times 4 = 36$, $10 \times 4 = 40$, $11 \times 4 = 44$, $12 \times 4 = 48$

2. $1 \times 8 = 8$, $2 \times 8 = 16$, $3 \times 8 = 24$, $4 \times 8 = 32$, $5 \times 8 = 40$, $6 \times 8 = 48$, $7 \times 8 = 56$, $8 \times 8 = 64$, $9 \times 8 = 72$, $10 \times 8 = 80$, $11 \times 8 = 88$, $12 \times 8 = 96$

3. $1 \times 12 = 12$, $2 \times 12 = 24$, $3 \times 12 = 36$, $4 \times 12 = 48$, $5 \times 12 = 60$, $6 \times 12 = 72$, $7 \times 12 = 84$, $8 \times 12 = 96$, $9 \times 12 = 108$, $10 \times 12 = 120$, $11 \times 12 = 132$, $12 \times 12 = 144$

4. 12, 3, 48, 2, 40, 9, 84, 24, 5, 7, 72, 24, 5, 16, 12

Activities

1. 6×12 and 72, 11×4 and 44, 4×8 and 32, 7×8 and 56, 6×4 and 24, 9×6 and 54, 8×12 and 96, 11×8 and 88

2. 8, 12, 20, 24, 28;
32, 48, 56, 72;
24, 48, 72, 84

3. £48, £80, £20, £28, £16, £24

4. 24, 96, $12 \times 8 = 96$, $5 \times 12 = 60$, $9 \times 8 = 72$, $7 \times 12 = 84$

5. Path drawn through: 64, 56, 84, 48, 16, 96, 72, 36, 120, 24, 16, 144

6. 32, £60, 84, 12, 144, true, 8, 16

7. ✔, ✔, ✔, ✗, ✗, ✔, ✗, ✔

8. elephant

Five, seven and eleven times tables

Tables practice

1. $1 \times 5 = 5$, $2 \times 5 = 10$, $3 \times 5 = 15$, $4 \times 5 = 20$, $5 \times 5 = 25$, $6 \times 5 = 30$, $7 \times 5 = 35$, $8 \times 5 = 40$, $9 \times 5 = 45$, $10 \times 5 = 50$, $11 \times 5 = 55$, $12 \times 5 = 60$

2. $1 \times 7 = 7$, $2 \times 7 = 14$, $3 \times 7 = 21$, $4 \times 7 = 28$, $5 \times 7 = 35$, $6 \times 7 = 42$, $7 \times 7 = 49$, $8 \times 7 = 56$, $9 \times 7 = 63$, $10 \times 7 = 70$, $11 \times 7 = 77$, $12 \times 7 = 84$

3. $1 \times 11 = 11$, $2 \times 11 = 22$, $3 \times 11 = 33$, $4 \times 11 = 44$, $5 \times 11 = 55$, $6 \times 11 = 66$, $7 \times 11 = 77$, $8 \times 11 = 88$, $9 \times 11 = 99$, $10 \times 11 = 110$, $11 \times 11 = 121$, $12 \times 11 = 132$

4. 30, 12, 70, 3, 25, 8, 55, 14, 8, 12, 99, 56, 7, 35, 10

Activities

1. A = 42, B = 60, C = 30, D = 28, E = 35, F = 33

2. £20, £88, £77, £25, £63, £84

3. 42, 121, 7, 56, false, 12, 66

4. 10, 15, 25, 30;
7, 21, 28, 42;
22, 33, 55, 66;
55, 50, 40, 35;
77, 63, 49;
132, 110, 99, 77

5. Shade 63, 15, 84, 25, 49, 10, 70, 66, 50, 56, 45, 21, 88; letter N

6. Blue – 7, 14, 21, 28, 35, 42, 49, 56, 63, 70, 77, 84; Yellow – 11, 22, 33, 44, 55, 66, 77, 88; 77 circled twice

7. Circle 3×7, 11×6, 11×11, 9×3, 12×7

8. $8 \times 7 = 56$, $12 \times 5 = 60$, $11 \times 11 = 121$

9. They are all animals: goat, calf, horse, lamb

Odd times tables

Tables practice

1. 30, 5, 8, 3, 110, 12, 49, 21, 18, 2, 50, 5, 9, 35, 7, 12, 54, 99, 7, 44, 8, 70, 33, 9, 7, 22, 40, 5, 9, 21, 24, 4, 77, 9, 56, 5, 4, 3, 5, 1, 33, 42, 11, 2, 12, 3, 6, 66, 10, 84, 63

Activities

1. £44, 35, 56, 6, £66

2. Red – 9, 18, 27, 36, 45, 54, 63, 72, 81, 90, 99; blue – 11, 22, 33, 44, 55, 66, 77, 88, 99; 99 circled twice

3. 55, 27, 6, 12, false, 121

Even times tables

Tables practice

1. 24, 3, 9, 6, 12, 4, 24, 48, 36, 5, 56, 7, 6, 40, 32, 60, 84, 70, 8, 14, 2, 32, 48, 18, 6,

Answers

42, 28, 12, 3, 30, 120, 5, 64, 11, 36, 3, 6, 1, 72, 5, 44, 54, 36, 3, 6, 16, 9, 110, 20, 80, 96

Activities

1. £6, £24, £60, £64, £24, £28, 6, 9
2. 14, 12 × 6 = 72, 5 × 12 = 60

Mixed times tables

Activities

1.

(×1) 3, 4, 5, 6, 7, 8, 9, 10, 11, 12;
(×2) 2, 4, 6, 8, 10, 14, 16, 18, 20, 22, 24;
(×3) 3, 6, 12, 15, 18, 21, 24, 27, 30, 33, 36;
(×4) 4, 8, 12, 16, 24, 28, 32, 36, 40, 44, 48;
(×5) 5, 10, 15, 20, 25, 30, 35, 45, 50, 55, 60;
(×6) 6, 12, 18, 24, 30, 36, 48, 54, 60, 66, 72;
(×7) 7, 14, 21, 28, 35, 42, 49, 56, 63, 70, 84;
(×8) 8, 16, 24, 32, 40, 48, 56, 64, 80, 88, 96;
(×9) 9, 18, 36, 45, 54, 63, 72, 81, 90, 99, 108;
(×10) 10, 20, 30, 40, 60, 70, 80, 90, 100, 110, 120;
(×11) 11, 22, 33, 44, 55, 66, 77, 99, 110, 121, 132;
(×12) 12, 24, 36, 60, 72, 84, 96, 108, 120, 132, 144

2. 12, 24, 66, 20, 56, 108, 14, 20, 144, 72, 42, 27, 132, 32
3. Priya (red) – 15, 35, 60; Sam (blue) – 18, 27, 54, 72; Georgia (green) – 44, 66, 77, 88, 132; Georgia bursts the most balloons
4. 5 people – 5, 10, 40, 20; 8 people – 8, 16, 64, 32; 12 people – 12, 24, 96, 48
5. Orange (fives) – 40, 15, 25, 55; red (sixes) 12, 66, 42, 54, 24; blue (sevens) – 14, 49, 42, 21, 7; green (nines) – 81, 99, 27, 54; 42 and 54 circled in more than one colour
6. 7 chests – 35, 49, 77, 84; 11 chests – 55, 77, 121, 132; 6 chests – 30, 42, 66, 72
7. 12 × 4 = 48, 6 × 8 = 48, 4 × 12 = 48; 6 × 4 = 24, 3 × 8 = 24, 2 × 12 = 24; 12 × 8 = 96, 8 × 12 = 96
8. 5, 3, 7
9. pink – 6 × 3, yellow – 3 × 12 and 9 × 4, red 7 × 6 and 6 × 7, brown 9 × 8 and 12 × 6, purple 12 × 9
10. practice makes perfect
11. Circle 12 × 4 and 6 × 8, 9 × 6 and 6 × 9, 7 × 3, 10 × 11, 12 × 11

12. 42, 48, 48, 40, 72, 132; 3 ways: 12 small, 9 medium or 6 large
13. 6, 9, 11, 11, 9, 9, 7, 7, 9, 9, 11, 4
14. Snake beginning 5: 10, 15, 20, 25, 30, 35, 40, 45, 50, 55, 60
    Snake beginning 7: 14, 21, 28, 35, 42, 49, 56, 63, 70, 77, 84
    Snake beginning 9: 18, 27, 36, 45, 54, 63, 72, 81, 90
    Snake beginning 11: 22, 33, 44, 55, 66, 77, 88, 99
15. 11, 8 × 7 = 56, 8 × 9 = 72, 3 × 7 = 21, 5 × 9 = 45, 12 × 9 = 108

Speed tests

Test 1

6, 21, 32, 35, 72, 84, 32, 108, 110, 99, 60, 36, 40, 24, 35, 48, 54, 100, 121, 132, 24, 22, 120, 27, 36, 77, 54, 30, 40, 12, 4, 24, 8, 28, 25, 18, 42, 40, 36, 90

Test 2

33, 48, 12, 15, 48, 45, 30, 49, 64, 99, 60, 66, 84, 144, 132, 20, 63, 56, 63, 42, 24, 9, 14, 108, 88, 80, 81, 72, 56, 36, 60, 44, 18, 16, 36, 77, 70, 72, 16, 70

Test 3

12, 45, 27, 28, 72, 24, 15, 80, 10, 60, 22, 5, 96, 12, 144, 90, 30, 14, 20, 33, 120, 8, 55, 16, 24, 21, 66, 12, 20, 6, 77, 50, 18, 36, 50, 18, 48, 88, 10, 20

Multiplication grids

Grid 1

8	4	9	3	11
16	8	18	6	22
24	12	27	9	33
32	16	36	12	44
40	20	45	15	55
48	24	54	18	66
56	28	63	21	77
64	32	72	24	88
72	36	81	27	99
80	40	90	30	110
88	44	99	33	121
96	48	108	36	132

Grid 2

28	20	48	24	40
42	30	72	36	60
77	55	132	66	110
14	10	24	12	20
84	60	144	72	120
63	45	108	54	90
35	25	60	30	50
7	5	12	6	10
21	15	36	18	30
49	35	84	42	70
70	50	120	60	100
56	40	96	48	80

Test your tables

1. Write out the twelve times table.

1 × 12 = ☐

2 × 12 = ☐

☐ × ☐ = ☐

☐ × ☐ = ☐

☐ × ☐ = ☐

☐ × ☐ = ☐

☐ × ☐ = ☐

☐ × ☐ = ☐

☐ × ☐ = ☐

☐ × ☐ = ☐

☐ × ☐ = ☐

☐ × ☐ = ☐

2. Complete these multiplication facts.

☐ × 12 = 60

4 × 12 = ☐

2 × 12 = ☐

10 × 12 = ☐

12 × 12 = ☐

☐ × 12 = 108

☐ × 12 = 72

8 × 12 = ☐

☐ × 12 = 84

☐ × 12 = 12

3 × 12 = ☐

☐ × 12 = 132

Score /12

Score /12

Three, six and nine times tables

1. Write out the three times table as quickly as you can.

1 × 3 = ☐   2 × 3 = ☐   ☐ × ☐ = ☐

☐ × ☐ = ☐   ☐ × ☐ = ☐   ☐ × ☐ = ☐

☐ × ☐ = ☐   ☐ × ☐ = ☐   ☐ × ☐ = ☐

☐ × ☐ = ☐   ☐ × ☐ = ☐   ☐ × ☐ = ☐

2. Write out the six times table as quickly as you can.

1 × 6 = ☐   2 × 6 = ☐   ☐ × ☐ = ☐

☐ × ☐ = ☐   ☐ × ☐ = ☐   ☐ × ☐ = ☐

☐ × ☐ = ☐   ☐ × ☐ = ☐   ☐ × ☐ = ☐

☐ × ☐ = ☐   ☐ × ☐ = ☐   ☐ × ☐ = ☐

3. Write out the nine times table as quickly as you can.

1 × 9 = ☐   2 × 9 = ☐   ☐ × ☐ = ☐

☐ × ☐ = ☐   ☐ × ☐ = ☐   ☐ × ☐ = ☐

☐ × ☐ = ☐   ☐ × ☐ = ☐   ☐ × ☐ = ☐

☐ × ☐ = ☐   ☐ × ☐ = ☐   ☐ × ☐ = ☐

4. Write in the missing number to complete each multiplication fact.

6 × 3 = ☐   ☐ × 9 = 36   10 × 9 = ☐

☐ × 6 = 72   5 × 6 = ☐   ☐ × 9 = 108

5 × 9 = ☐   2 × 3 = ☐   ☐ × 3 = 33

☐ × 3 = 15   9 × 9 = ☐   8 × 3 = ☐

☐ × 9 = 18   7 × 6 = ☐   ☐ × 6 = 12

Three, six and nine times tables

Activities

1. Fill in the missing multiplications and answers to make the two pyramids match. Use only multiplications from the three, six, and nine times tables. The top brick in each pyramid has been done for you.

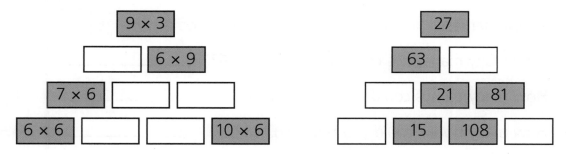

2. Use the stepping stones to find the path across the river. You can only step on the stones that are answers in the six or nine times tables. Colour the path you used.

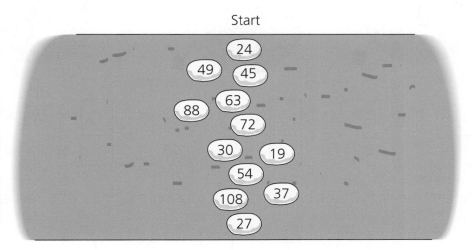

3. Answer these questions.

   What are three sixes?   _____

   What is the seventh multiple of 9?   _____

   How many threes in 27?   _____

   What is 9 multiplied by itself?   _____

   What is 6 doubled?   _____

   What is 12 multiplied by 3?   _____

4. A shop sells magazines for £3, games for £6 and books for £9.

Write down how much it costs for:

Eight magazines   £ ☐   Seven games   £ ☐

Four books   £ ☐   Five magazines   £ ☐

Twelve games   £ ☐   Eleven books   £ ☐

How many magazines could you buy for £36? _____

How many games could you buy for £54? _____

How many books could you buy for £108? _____

5. Complete the multiplication facts for the scores on each target board.

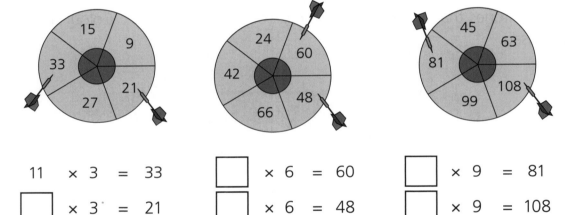

11 × 3 = 33   ☐ × 6 = 60   ☐ × 9 = 81

☐ × 3 = 21   ☐ × 6 = 48   ☐ × 9 = 108

6. Complete the sequences by writing the missing multiples of three, six or nine.

12	☐	☐	21	☐	27	☐
27	☐	45	☐	☐	72	☐
☐	33	☐	☐	☐	21	☐
81	☐	☐	54	☐	36	☐
18	☐	30	☐	☐	48	☐
☐	66	☐	☐	☐	42	☐

7. Choose the correct answer for each multiplication. Circle the letter next to that answer.

4 × 6 =	24 **G** or 27 **R**	4 × 9 =	36 **I** or 43 **A**
9 × 9 =	78 **D** or 81 **N**	3 × 6 =	18 **E** or 16 **B**
6 × 3 =	15 **S** or 18 **E**	12 × 9 =	108 **T** or 105 **F**
7 × 6 =	52 **M** or 42 **H**	2 × 9 =	15 **C** or 18 **E**

Rearrange the letters you have circled to spell out a number that is a multiple of three, six and nine. What is the number? _____

8. Draw a line to join each multiplication to the correct answer.

(7 × 3) (8 × 6) (7 × 9) (12 × 3) (4 × 6) (12 × 9) (12 × 6)

| 72 | | 63 | | 21 | | 108 | | 36 | | 48 | | 24 |

9. Use the clues to complete the cross-number grid. The last digit of each answer is the first digit of the next answer. The first answer has been done for you.

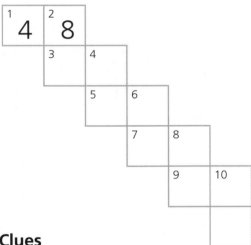

Clues

(1) 8 × 6
(2) 9 × 9
(3) 4 × 3
(4) 4 × 6
(5) 5 × 9

(6) 9 × 6
(7) 7 × 6
(8) 9 × 3
(9) 12 × 6
(10) 7 × 3

Four, eight and twelve times tables

Tables practice

1. Write out the four times table as quickly as you can.

1 × 4 = ☐ 2 × 4 = ☐ ☐ × ☐ = ☐
☐ × ☐ = ☐ ☐ × ☐ = ☐ ☐ × ☐ = ☐
☐ × ☐ = ☐ ☐ × ☐ = ☐ ☐ × ☐ = ☐
☐ × ☐ = ☐ ☐ × ☐ = ☐ ☐ × ☐ = ☐

2. Write out the eight times table as quickly as you can.

1 × 8 = ☐ 2 × 8 = ☐ ☐ × ☐ = ☐
☐ × ☐ = ☐ ☐ × ☐ = ☐ ☐ × ☐ = ☐
☐ × ☐ = ☐ ☐ × ☐ = ☐ ☐ × ☐ = ☐
☐ × ☐ = ☐ ☐ × ☐ = ☐ ☐ × ☐ = ☐

3. Write out the twelve times table as quickly as you can.

1 × 12 = ☐ 2 × 12 = ☐ ☐ × ☐ = ☐
☐ × ☐ = ☐ ☐ × ☐ = ☐ ☐ × ☐ = ☐
☐ × ☐ = ☐ ☐ × ☐ = ☐ ☐ × ☐ = ☐
☐ × ☐ = ☐ ☐ × ☐ = ☐ ☐ × ☐ = ☐

4. Write in the missing numbers to complete each multiplication fact.

3 × 4 = ☐   ☐ × 12 = 36   6 × 8 = ☐
☐ × 8 = 16   5 × 8 = ☐   ☐ × 12 = 108
7 × 12 = ☐   2 × 12 = ☐   ☐ × 8 = 40
☐ × 4 = 28   9 × 8 = ☐   6 × 4 = ☐
☐ × 12 = 60   4 × 4 = ☐   ☐ × 12 = 144

Four, eight and twelve times tables

Activities

1. Each key opens a door with the matching multiple. Draw lines to join each key to the correct door.

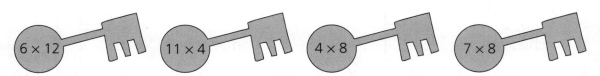

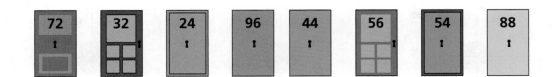

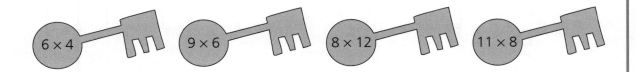

2. Write the numbers on the shirts by counting on in fours, eights or twelves.

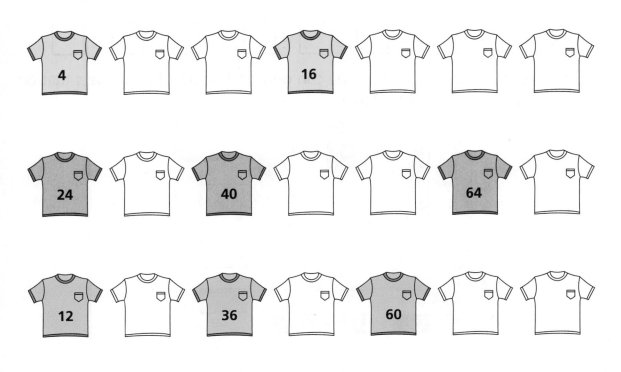

3. A theme park ride ticket costs £8 for adults and £4 for children.

Write down how much it costs for:

6 adult tickets   £ ☐   10 adult tickets   £ ☐

5 child tickets   £ ☐   7 child tickets   £ ☐

4 child tickets   £ ☐   3 adult tickets   £ ☐

4. If an arrow lands in the white ring of the target it scores 8 times the number. If the arrow lands in the red ring it scores 12 times the number. Write down the multiplication fact for each target board.

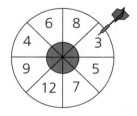      

3 × 8 = ☐   8 × 12 = ☐   ☐ × ☐ = ☐

☐ × ☐ = ☐   ☐ × ☐ = ☐   ☐ × ☐ = ☐

5. Find a path through the maze. You can only go through the numbers that are in the eight or twelve times tables.

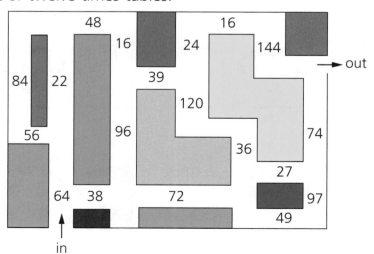

6. Answer these questions.

What is 8 × 4? _____

A bag costs £12. How much would it cost for 5 bags? £ _____

What is the seventh multiple of 12? _____

What number multiplied by 8 gives the answer 96? _____

What is 12 multiplied by itself? _____

The seventh multiple of 8 is 56. True or false? _____

How many eights in 64? _____

What is the fourth multiple of 4? _____

7. Some of these tables facts are correct and some are not. Tick those with correct answers. Put a cross next to those that are wrong.

6 × 4 = 24 ☐   8 × 8 = 64 ☐

10 × 12 = 120 ☐   4 × 4 = 18 ☐

11 × 8 = 89 ☐   6 × 12 = 72 ☐

3 × 4 = 16 ☐   12 × 8 = 96 ☐

8. Work out the answer to the multiplication in each flower. Use your answers to fill in the missing letters in the spaces below.

| 9 × 12 | 11 × 4 | 4 × 12 | 7 × 8 | 11 × 12 | 6 × 4 | 8 × 8 |
| a | h | l | e | t | n | p |

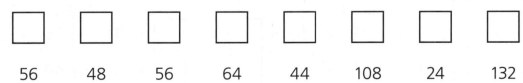

☐ ☐ ☐ ☐ ☐ ☐ ☐ ☐

56   48   56   64   44   108   24   132

What is the hidden animal? _____

Five, seven and eleven times tables

Tables practice

1. Write out the five times table as quickly as you can.

1 × 5 = ☐   2 × 5 = ☐   ☐ × ☐ = ☐

☐ × ☐ = ☐   ☐ × ☐ = ☐   ☐ × ☐ = ☐

☐ × ☐ = ☐   ☐ × ☐ = ☐   ☐ × ☐ = ☐

☐ × ☐ = ☐   ☐ × ☐ = ☐   ☐ × ☐ = ☐

2. Write out the seven times table as quickly as you can.

1 × 7 = ☐   2 × 7 = ☐   ☐ × ☐ = ☐

☐ × ☐ = ☐   ☐ × ☐ = ☐   ☐ × ☐ = ☐

☐ × ☐ = ☐   ☐ × ☐ = ☐   ☐ × ☐ = ☐

☐ × ☐ = ☐   ☐ × ☐ = ☐   ☐ × ☐ = ☐

3. Write out the eleven times table as quickly as you can.

1 × 11 = ☐   2 × 11 = ☐   ☐ × ☐ = ☐

☐ × ☐ = ☐   ☐ × ☐ = ☐   ☐ × ☐ = ☐

☐ × ☐ = ☐   ☐ × ☐ = ☐   ☐ × ☐ = ☐

☐ × ☐ = ☐   ☐ × ☐ = ☐   ☐ × ☐ = ☐

4. Write in the missing numbers to complete each multiplication fact.

6 × 5 = ☐   ☐ × 11 = 132   10 × 7 = ☐

☐ × 7 = 21   5 × 5 = ☐   ☐ × 11 = 88

5 × 11 = ☐   2 × 7 = ☐   ☐ × 5 = 40

☐ × 5 = 60   9 × 11 = ☐   8 × 7 = ☐

☐ × 7 = 49   7 × 5 = ☐   ☐ × 11 = 110

Five, seven and eleven times tables

Activities

1. Follow the tunnel each mole will take to reach its burrow. Write the answer to the multiplication in the mole's burrow.

2. A small pizza costs £5. A medium pizza costs £7. A large pizza costs £11.

   Write down how much it costs for:

   4 small pizzas   £ ☐   8 large pizzas   £ ☐

   7 large pizzas   £ ☐   5 small pizzas   £ ☐

   9 medium pizzas   £ ☐   12 medium pizzas £ ☐

3. Answer these questions.

   What is the sixth multiple of 7?   _____

   What is 11 multiplied by itself?   _____

   How many fives in 35?   _____

   What is 8 times 7?   _____

   Twelve elevens are 133. True or false?   _____

   What do you need to multiply by 5 to get 60?   _____

   What is the product of 6 and 11?   _____

4. Fill in the missing numbers by counting on or back in fives, sevens or elevens.

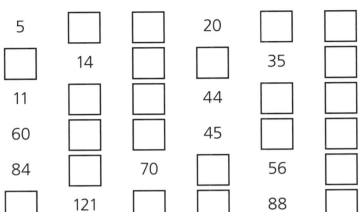

5. Shade the multiples of five, seven or eleven. Which letter can you see? ☐

49	48	69	81	88
25	10	12	96	21
84	6	70	17	45
15	13	54	66	56
63	31	19	41	50

6. Look at the number grid. Circle all the multiples of seven in blue and all the multiples of eleven in yellow. Which number have you circled twice? ☐

1	2	3	4	5	6	7	8	9	10
11	12	13	14	15	16	17	18	19	20
21	22	23	24	25	26	27	28	29	30
31	32	33	34	35	36	37	38	39	40
41	42	43	44	45	46	47	48	49	50
51	52	53	54	55	56	57	58	59	60
61	62	63	64	65	66	67	68	69	70
71	72	73	74	75	76	77	78	79	80
81	82	83	84	85	86	87	88	89	90

Five, seven and eleven times tables

7. Circle the multiplication that matches the number in the box.

| 21 | 5 × 4 | 2 × 7 | 4 × 11 | 3 × 7 |

| 66 | 12 × 5 | 8 × 7 | 11 × 6 | 9 × 5 |

| 121 | 5 × 12 | 11 × 11 | 7 × 12 | 11 × 10 |

| 27 | 4 × 7 | 11 × 3 | 9 × 3 | 5 × 5 |

| 84 | 11 × 8 | 12 × 3 | 8 × 3 | 12 × 7 |

8. Look at the numbers in the circles. Write the multiplication by 5, 7 or 11 that gives you that number.

56

60

121

☐ × ☐ = ☐   ☐ × ☐ = ☐   ☐ × ☐ = ☐

9. Work out the answer to each times tables fact to complete the grid.

6 × 5		s
3 × 7		h
4 × 11		e
8 × 11		g
6 × 7		o
7 × 5		t

5 × 11		c
9 × 7		a
12 × 11		l
10 × 7		f
9 × 5		m
6 × 11		b
12 × 7		r

Using the code above, replace each of the numbers with the correct letters.

☐ ☐ ☐ ☐
88 42 63 35

☐ ☐ ☐ ☐
55 63 132 70

☐ ☐ ☐ ☐ ☐
21 42 84 30 44

☐ ☐ ☐ ☐
132 63 45 66

What do all the answers have in common? _____

Odd times tables

1. Write in the missing number to complete each multiplication fact.

10 × 3 = ☐   ☐ × 9 = 45   ☐ × 9 = 72

☐ × 5 = 15   10 × 11 = ☐   ☐ × 11 = 132

7 × 7 = ☐   7 × 3 = ☐   6 × 3 = ☐

☐ × 9 = 18   10 × 5 = ☐   ☐ × 5 = 25

☐ × 11 = 99   5 × 7 = ☐   1 × 7 = ☐

4 × 3 = ☐   6 × 9 = ☐   11 × 9 = ☐

☐ × 5 = 35   4 × 11 = ☐   ☐ × 11 = 88

10 × 7 = ☐   11 × 3 = ☐   3 × 3 = ☐

☐ × 9 = 63   2 × 11 = ☐   8 × 5 = ☐

☐ × 11 = 55   ☐ × 3 = 27   3 × 7 = ☐

8 × 3 = ☐   ☐ × 5 = 20   7 × 11 = ☐

☐ × 5 = 45   8 × 7 = ☐   ☐ × 3 = 15

☐ × 7 = 28   ☐ × 9 = 27   1 × 5 = ☐

☐ × 9 = 9   3 × 11 = ☐   6 × 7 = ☐

1 × 11 = ☐   ☐ × 3 = 6   ☐ × 9 = 108

1 × 3 = ☐   ☐ × 5 = 30   6 × 11 = ☐

2 × 5 = ☐   12 × 7 = ☐   9 × 7 = ☐

Activities

1. It costs £11 to hire a taxi. The taxi can carry five people and seven bags.

   How much would it cost to hire 4 taxis? £ ☐

   How many people can 7 taxis carry? ☐

   How many bags can 8 taxis carry? ☐

   A group of 30 people needs to hire taxis.

   How many taxis would they need? ☐

   How much would it cost? £ ☐

2. Look at the number grid.

   Circle all the multiples of nine in red and all the multiples of eleven in blue.

   Which number have you circled twice? ☐

1	2	3	4	5	6	7	8	9	10
11	12	13	14	15	16	17	18	19	20
21	22	23	24	25	26	27	28	29	30
31	32	33	34	35	36	37	38	39	40
41	42	43	44	45	46	47	48	49	50
51	52	53	54	55	56	57	58	59	60
61	62	63	64	65	66	67	68	69	70
71	72	73	74	75	76	77	78	79	80
81	82	83	84	85	86	87	88	89	90
91	92	93	94	95	96	97	98	99	100

3. Answer these questions.

   What is the fifth multiple of 11? _____

   What is the product of 3 and 9? _____

   What do you need to multiply 7 by to get 42? _____

   Which number multiplied by 9 is 108? _____

   7×3 is 24. True or false? _____

   What is 11 multiplied by itself? _____

Even times tables

Tables practice

1. Write in the missing numbers to complete each multiplication fact.

$12 \times 2 = \boxed{}$ $\boxed{} \times 2 = 6$ $\boxed{} \times 12 = 108$

$\boxed{} \times 4 = 24$ $3 \times 4 = \boxed{}$ $\boxed{} \times 2 = 8$

$4 \times 6 = \boxed{}$ $8 \times 6 = \boxed{}$ $9 \times 4 = \boxed{}$

$\boxed{} \times 8 = 40$ $7 \times 8 = \boxed{}$ $\boxed{} \times 6 = 42$

$\boxed{} \times 10 = 60$ $4 \times 10 = \boxed{}$ $4 \times 8 = \boxed{}$

$5 \times 12 = \boxed{}$ $7 \times 12 = \boxed{}$ $7 \times 10 = \boxed{}$

$\boxed{} \times 2 = 16$ $7 \times 2 = \boxed{}$ $\boxed{} \times 12 = 24$

$8 \times 4 = \boxed{}$ $12 \times 4 = \boxed{}$ $9 \times 2 = \boxed{}$

$\boxed{} \times 6 = 36$ $7 \times 6 = \boxed{}$ $7 \times 4 = \boxed{}$

$\boxed{} \times 8 = 96$ $\boxed{} \times 8 = 24$ $5 \times 6 = \boxed{}$

$12 \times 10 = \boxed{}$ $\boxed{} \times 10 = 50$ $8 \times 8 = \boxed{}$

$\boxed{} \times 12 = 132$ $3 \times 12 = \boxed{}$ $\boxed{} \times 10 = 30$

$\boxed{} \times 2 = 12$ $\boxed{} \times 2 = 2$ $6 \times 12 = \boxed{}$

$\boxed{} \times 4 = 20$ $11 \times 4 = \boxed{}$ $9 \times 6 = \boxed{}$

$6 \times 6 = \boxed{}$ $\boxed{} \times 6 = 18$ $\boxed{} \times 8 = 48$

$2 \times 8 = \boxed{}$ $\boxed{} \times 8 = 72$ $11 \times 10 = \boxed{}$

$2 \times 10 = \boxed{}$ $8 \times 10 = \boxed{}$ $8 \times 12 = \boxed{}$

Activities

1. Here are some items for sale in a sports shop.

Sports bag	£12
Boots	£10
Shirt	£8
Shorts	£4
Socks	£2
Football	£6

Write down how much it costs to buy:

Three pairs of socks £ ☐   Four footballs £ ☐

Six pairs of boots £ ☐   Eight shirts £ ☐

Two sports bags £ ☐   Seven shorts £ ☐

How many sports bags could you buy for £72? _____

How many footballs could you buy for £54? _____

2. Below are some targets.

   If an arrow lands in the white ring it scores twice the number.

   If an arrow lands in the blue ring it scores six times the number.

   If an arrow lands in the red ring it scores twelve times the number.

   Write the multiplication fact for each target.

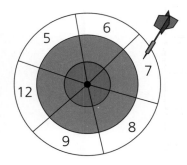

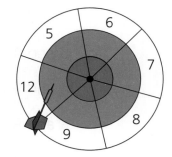

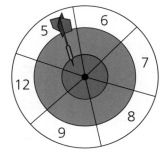

7 × 2 = ☐   ☐ × ☐ = ☐   ☐ × ☐ = ☐

Mixed times tables

1. Complete the full multiplication grid.

×	1	2	3	4	5	6	7	8	9	10	11	12
1	1	2										
2						12						
3			9									
4					20							
5								40				
6							42					
7											77	
8									72			
9			27									
10					50							
11								88				
12				48								

2. Find the product of the following:

3 and 4	☐		4 and 6	☐
6 and 11	☐		10 and 2	☐
8 and 7	☐		9 and 12	☐
7 and 2	☐		5 and 4	☐
12 and 12	☐		8 and 9	☐
7 and 6	☐		3 and 9	☐
11 and 12	☐		8 and 4	☐

3. Priya, Sam and Georgia are bursting balloons.

Priya can only burst balloons which are multiples of five.

Sam can only burst balloons which are multiples of nine.

Georgia can only burst balloons which are multiples of eleven.

Colour Priya's balloons red, Sam's balloons blue and Georgia's balloons green.

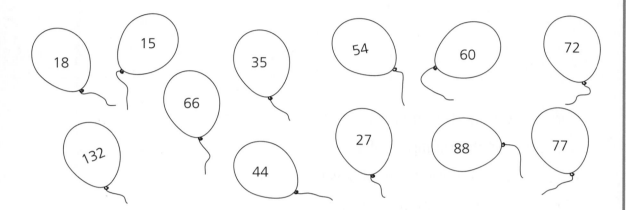

Who bursts the most balloons? _____

4. Here is a recipe. It makes a fruit salad for one person.

| 1 apple |
| 2 kiwi fruit |
| 8 blueberries |
| 4 strawberries |

Write down what you would need to make a fruit salad for:

5	**people**	**8**	**people**	**12**	**people**
☐	apples	☐	apples	☐	apples
☐	kiwi fruit	☐	kiwi fruit	☐	kiwi fruit
☐	blueberries	☐	blueberries	☐	blueberries
☐	strawberries	☐	strawberries	☐	strawberries

5. Look at the numbers below.

81	14	40	12	15
66	99	49	42	27	54
25	21	55	24	7

Circle in orange the multiples of five.

Circle in red the multiples of six.

Circle in blue the multiples of seven.

Circle in green the multiples of nine.

Which numbers have been circled in more than one colour? _____

6. A treasure chest contains: Five emeralds   Seven rubies

Eleven diamonds   Twelve sapphires

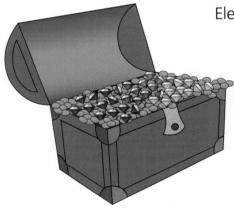

Write down how jewels there are in:

7 treasure chests   **11 treasure chests**   **6 treasure chests**

☐ emeralds   ☐ emeralds   ☐ emeralds

☐ rubies   ☐ rubies   ☐ rubies

☐ diamonds   ☐ diamonds   ☐ diamonds

☐ sapphires   ☐ sapphires   ☐ sapphires

7. For each number write a different multiplication fact from the four, eight or twelve times table.

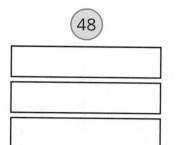   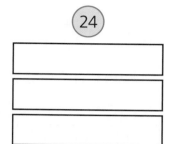   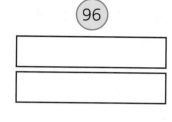

8. Here are some number machines. Fill in the missing numbers on the machines.

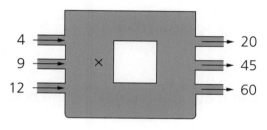   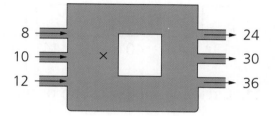

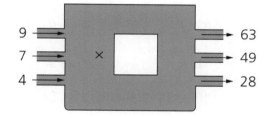

9. Work out the answer for each multiplication. Use your answers to find the colour in the key and colour the picture.

Key   18 = pink, 36 = yellow, 42 = red, 72 = brown, 108 = purple

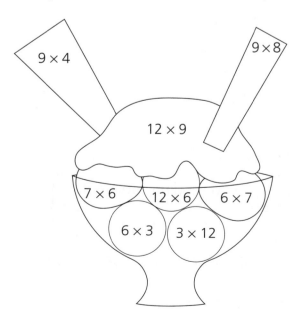

Mixed times tables

10. Work out the answer to the multiplication in each bubble. Use your answers to fill in the missing letters in the spaces below. What is the hidden message?

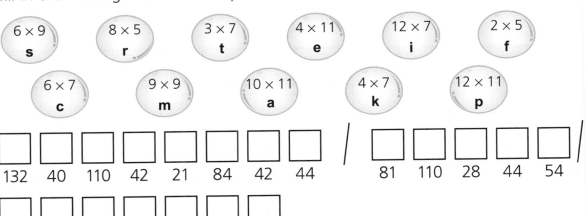

6 × 9	8 × 5	3 × 7	4 × 11	12 × 7	2 × 5
s	**r**	**t**	**e**	**i**	**f**

6 × 7	9 × 9	10 × 11	4 × 7	12 × 11
c	**m**	**a**	**k**	**p**

☐ ☐ ☐ ☐ ☐ ☐ ☐ ☐ / ☐ ☐ ☐ ☐ ☐ /
132 40 110 42 21 84 42 44   81 110 28 44 54

☐ ☐ ☐ ☐ ☐ ☐ ☐
132 44 40 10 44 42 21

11. Circle the multiplication or multiplications that match the number in the box.

48	12 × 4	6 × 6	6 × 8	7 × 12
54	9 × 6	5 × 7	5 × 8	6 × 9
21	3 × 12	4 × 7	7 × 3	9 × 6
110	9 × 5	10 × 11	12 × 12	8 × 8
132	10 × 12	12 × 11	5 × 7	9 × 9

12. Pencils are packed in different-sized boxes.

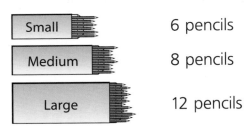

Small — 6 pencils

Medium — 8 pencils

Large — 12 pencils

Write down how many pencils there are in:

7 small boxes ☐   6 medium boxes ☐   4 large boxes ☐

5 medium boxes ☐   12 small boxes ☐   11 large boxes ☐

How many different ways can 72 pencils be packed?

13. Complete the multiplication facts.

48 = ☐ × 8   36 = ☐ × 4   99 = ☐ × 9

55 = ☐ × 5   72 = ☐ × 8   18 = ☐ × 2

77 = ☐ × 11   49 = ☐ × 7   27 = ☐ × 3

54 = ☐ × 6   110 = ☐ × 10   32 = ☐ × 8

14. Write the multiples for five, seven, nine and eleven to complete the snakes.

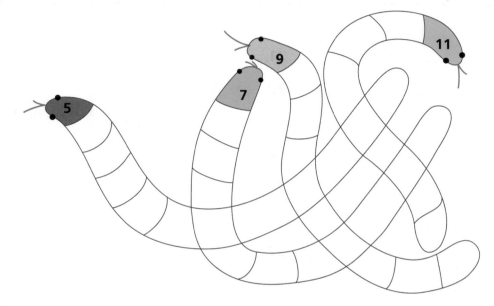

15. Look at the answer on each calculator. Write the multiplication by four, seven or nine that gives that answer.

☐ × 4 = 44   ☐ × ☐ = 56   ☐ × ☐ = ☐

☐ × ☐ = ☐   ☐ × ☐ = ☐   ☐ × ☐ = ☐

Speed test

- How many of these can you complete correctly in 2 minutes?
- Write your answers on paper. Number them 1 to 40.
- Don't worry if you cannot answer them all, just answer them as quickly as you can.
- Stop after 2 minutes, check your answers and record your score on the progress chart opposite.
- Then, try again at another time to see if you can improve your results!

Test 1

1. $3 \times 2 = $ _____

2. $7 \times 3 = $ _____

3. $8 \times 4 = $ _____

4. $7 \times 5 = $ _____

5. $12 \times 6 = $ _____

6. $12 \times 7 = $ _____

7. $4 \times 8 = $ _____

8. $12 \times 9 = $ _____

9. $11 \times 10 = $ _____

10. $9 \times 11 = $ _____

11. $5 \times 12 = $ _____

12. $9 \times 4 = $ _____

13. $8 \times 5 = $ _____

14. $6 \times 4 = $ _____

15. $5 \times 7 = $ _____

16. $6 \times 8 = $ _____

17. $6 \times 9 = $ _____

18. $10 \times 10 = $ _____

19. $11 \times 11 = $ _____

20. $11 \times 12 = $ _____

21. $2 \times 12 = $ _____

22. $2 \times 11 = $ _____

23. $12 \times 10 = $ _____

24. $3 \times 9 = $ _____

25. $6 \times 6 = $ _____

26. $11 \times 7 = $ _____

27. $9 \times 6 = $ _____

28. $6 \times 5 = $ _____

29. $10 \times 4 = $ _____

30. $4 \times 3 = $ _____

31. $2 \times 2 = $ _____

32. $8 \times 3 = $ _____

33. $4 \times 2 = $ _____

34. $7 \times 4 = $ _____

35. $5 \times 5 = $ _____

36. $3 \times 6 = $ _____

37. $6 \times 7 = $ _____

38. $5 \times 8 = $ _____

39. $4 \times 9 = $ _____

40. $9 \times 10 = $ _____

Progress chart

Colour in the stars to show your correct answers.

Attempt	**1**	**2**	**3**	**4**	**5**	**6**
Date	....	....	....	....	....	....

Scores out of 40

39 40	39 40	39 40	39 40	39 40	39 40
37 38	37 38	37 38	37 38	37 38	37 38
35 36	35 36	35 36	35 36	35 36	35 36
33 34	33 34	33 34	33 34	33 34	33 34
31 32	31 32	31 32	31 32	31 32	31 32
29 30	29 30	29 30	29 30	29 30	29 30
27 28	27 28	27 28	27 28	27 28	27 28
25 26	25 26	25 26	25 26	25 26	25 26
23 24	23 24	23 24	23 24	23 24	23 24
21 22	21 22	21 22	21 22	21 22	21 22
19 20	19 20	19 20	19 20	19 20	19 20
17 18	17 18	17 18	17 18	17 18	17 18
15 16	15 16	15 16	15 16	15 16	15 16
13 14	13 14	13 14	13 14	13 14	13 14
11 12	11 12	11 12	11 12	11 12	11 12
9 10	9 10	9 10	9 10	9 10	9 10
7 8	7 8	7 8	7 8	7 8	7 8
5 6	5 6	5 6	5 6	5 6	5 6
3 4	3 4	3 4	3 4	3 4	3 4
1 2	1 2	1 2	1 2	1 2	1 2

Speed test

- How many of these can you complete correctly in 2 minutes?
- Write your answers on paper. Number them 1 to 40.
- Don't worry if you cannot answer them all, just answer them as quickly as you can.
- Stop after 2 minutes, check your answers and record your score on the progress chart opposite.
- Then, try again at another time to see if you can improve your results!

Test 2

1. 3 × 11 = _____
2. 4 × 12 = _____
3. 6 × 2 = _____
4. 5 × 3 = _____
5. 12 × 4 = _____
6. 9 × 5 = _____
7. 5 × 6 = _____
8. 7 × 7 = _____
9. 8 × 8 = _____
10. 11 × 9 = _____
11. 6 × 10 = _____
12. 6 × 11 = _____
13. 7 × 12 = _____
14. 12 × 12 = _____
15. 12 × 11 = _____
16. 2 × 10 = _____
17. 7 × 9 = _____
18. 7 × 8 = _____
19. 9 × 7 = _____
20. 7 × 6 = _____

21. 6 × 4 = _____
22. 3 × 3 = _____
23. 7 × 2 = _____
24. 9 × 12 = _____
25. 8 × 11 = _____
26. 8 × 10 = _____
27. 9 × 9 = _____
28. 9 × 8 = _____
29. 8 × 7 = _____
30. 6 × 6 = _____
31. 12 × 5 = _____
32. 11 × 4 = _____
33. 6 × 3 = _____
34. 8 × 2 = _____
35. 3 × 12 = _____
36. 7 × 11 = _____
37. 7 × 10 = _____
38. 8 × 9 = _____
39. 2 × 8 = _____
40. 10 × 7 = _____

Progress chart

Colour in the stars to show your correct answers.

Attempt

	1	2	3	4	5	6

Date

Scores out of 40

39 40	39 40	39 40	39 40	39 40	39 40
37 38	37 38	37 38	37 38	37 38	37 38
35 36	35 36	35 36	35 36	35 36	35 36
33 34	33 34	33 34	33 34	33 34	33 34
31 32	31 32	31 32	31 32	31 32	31 32
29 30	29 30	29 30	29 30	29 30	29 30
27 28	27 28	27 28	27 28	27 28	27 28
25 26	25 26	25 26	25 26	25 26	25 26
23 24	23 24	23 24	23 24	23 24	23 24
21 22	21 22	21 22	21 22	21 22	21 22
19 20	19 20	19 20	19 20	19 20	19 20
17 18	17 18	17 18	17 18	17 18	17 18
15 16	15 16	15 16	15 16	15 16	15 16
13 14	13 14	13 14	13 14	13 14	13 14
11 12	11 12	11 12	11 12	11 12	11 12
9 10	9 10	9 10	9 10	9 10	9 10
7 8	7 8	7 8	7 8	7 8	7 8
5 6	5 6	5 6	5 6	5 6	5 6
3 4	3 4	3 4	3 4	3 4	3 4
1 2	1 2	1 2	1 2	1 2	1 2

Speed test

- How many of these can you complete correctly in 2 minutes?
- Write your answers on paper. Number them 1 to 40.
- Don't worry if you cannot answer them all, just answer them as quickly as you can.
- Stop after 2 minutes, check your answers and record your score on the progress chart opposite.
- Then, try again at another time to see if you can improve your results!

2:00:00

Test 3

1. 2 × 6 = _____

2. 5 × 9 = _____

3. 9 × 3 = _____

4. 4 × 7 = _____

5. 6 × 12 = _____

6. 3 × 8 = _____

7. 3 × 5 = _____

8. 10 × 8 = _____

9. 5 × 2 = _____

10. 10 × 6 = _____

11. 11 × 2 = _____

12. 1 × 5 = _____

13. 8 × 12 = _____

14. 3 × 4 = _____

15. 12 × 12 = _____

16. 10 × 9 = _____

17. 3 × 10 = _____

18. 2 × 7 = _____

19. 2 × 10 = _____

20. 11 × 3 = _____

21. 10 × 12 = _____

22. 2 × 4 = _____

23. 11 × 5 = _____

24. 4 × 4 = _____

25. 12 × 2 = _____

26. 3 × 7 = _____

27. 11 × 6 = _____

28. 6 × 2 = _____

29. 4 × 5 = _____

30. 2 × 3 = _____

31. 11 × 7 = _____

32. 5 × 10 = _____

33. 2 × 9 = _____

34. 12 × 3 = _____

35. 10 × 5 = _____

36. 9 × 2 = _____

37. 8 × 6 = _____

38. 11 × 8 = _____

39. 2 × 5 = _____

40. 5 × 4 = _____

Progress chart

Colour in the stars to show your correct answers.

| | Attempt 1 | Attempt 2 | Attempt 3 | Attempt 4 | Attempt 5 | Attempt 6 |

Attempt   1   2   3   4   5   6

Date ....

Scores out of 40

39	40	39	40	39	40	39	40	39	40	39	40
37	38	37	38	37	38	37	38	37	38	37	38
35	36	35	36	35	36	35	36	35	36	35	36
33	34	33	34	33	34	33	34	33	34	33	34
31	32	31	32	31	32	31	32	31	32	31	32
29	30	29	30	29	30	29	30	29	30	29	30
27	28	27	28	27	28	27	28	27	28	27	28
25	26	25	26	25	26	25	26	25	26	25	26
23	24	23	24	23	24	23	24	23	24	23	24
21	22	21	22	21	22	21	22	21	22	21	22
19	20	19	20	19	20	19	20	19	20	19	20
17	18	17	18	17	18	17	18	17	18	17	18
15	16	15	16	15	16	15	16	15	16	15	16
13	14	13	14	13	14	13	14	13	14	13	14
11	12	11	12	11	12	11	12	11	12	11	12
9	10	9	10	9	10	9	10	9	10	9	10
7	8	7	8	7	8	7	8	7	8	7	8
5	6	5	6	5	6	5	6	5	6	5	6
3	4	3	4	3	4	3	4	3	4	3	4
1	2	1	2	1	2	1	2	1	2	1	2

Multiplication grids

Complete the multiplication grids.

Grid 1

×	8	4	9	3	11
1					
2					
3					
4					
5					
6					
7					
8					
9					
10					
11					
12					

Grid 2

×	7	5	12	6	10
4					
6					
11					
2					
12					
9					
5					
1					
3					
7					
10					
8					